The Little Dog That Couldn't But Did!

A True Story of a Loveable Beagle Named Barney
(in his own words)

This is the true life story of Barney the Beagle, a medical pioneer in the field of pet mobility, a noted television personality, a connoisseur of fine foods, a dog who overcame countless obstacles life put in his path to become a valued member of his community and an inspiration to all who had the pleasure and good fortune to know him.

Published by Dockside Publishing
34 Dockside Court
Crossville, TN

Book design by Robert Reintsema

ISBN 978-1-4675-5300-1

Library of Congress catalog number: 2013932611

Born on a farm in rural West Virginia, I began life's journey as the runt of a litter of 11. It was a rocky start. Times were bad, and the farm's operators barely had enough food to feed themselves, let alone 11 new puppies. So at the age of 12 weeks, though still a mere tyke, I was told it was time to move on. An advertisement was placed in the local newspaper by the farm's owners. It read: "Any beagle puppy in the litter for $40."

This might sound vain, but in my opinion I was an adorable little dog. I was black, brown and white in color, with two big brown eyes that, while sad in nature, had a distinct charm. Though I was the smallest of the litter I was sure I was going to be one of the first puppies selected. Much to my dismay, I wasn't! It turned out I was one of the last.

It wasn't until a very nice couple came to the farm wanting to buy a male beagle puppy that my earlier optimism was rewarded.

They already had a four-year-old female beagle named Daisy but felt she was lonely and needed a young playmate. I was happy to join their family and become Daisy's younger brother. They named me Barney – Barney the Beagle.

They took me back to their cute little farmhouse some 30 miles away. On the drive home my new big sister wouldn't even look at me. She was obviously jealous. Apparently she feared I would be getting too much attention from my new parents; attention that she thought rightfully belonged to her.

My new home wasn't really what one would call a farm, as it was only two-and-a-half acres. My parents called it a "farmette." The house was very cozy and had a big front lawn to play in. It also had a small barn and a fenced-in pasture where my parents raised some steers, sheep and an occasional pig. Sometimes they allowed me and my sister, Daisy, to go with them to the barn and to run around in the pasture. I always had to be very careful where I stepped however, because you never knew what you might be *stepping in.*

My Cute and Cuddly Puppy Years

Big Sister Daisy   Daisy: My Mentor

The Farmhouse, My First Real Home

 The Barn: My Play House

More of My Puppy Pictures

My Teenage Years

I enjoyed life in the country. However, when I was two, my Dad took a new job in the city, and we had to move. Adjusting to city life was hard for my sister and me. Whenever we went out we were put on a leash. We couldn't run wherever we wanted as we did before. Not only that, but when we did go for a walk, it was on a sidewalk or a street. We missed not having any soft grass to walk or run on, but we had to adapt, and we did.

We lived in a nice big house. It had multiple levels, so we had to do a lot of climbing up and down stairs to get to where we wanted to go. At this point in my life, because I didn't get to go outside and run around as much as I had on the farm, I began to put on a lot of extra weight.

But I must confess, it wasn't just my inactivity that contributed to my "growing" problem; I also loved to eat! I guess you could say eating had become my obsession. Every waking moment I thought about food, and I suspect that when I slept, I dreamt about it as well. In fact, some folks took to calling me a "foodaholic."

If my biological parents could have seen me then, they wouldn't have believed their eyes. No longer was I the runt they remembered. As a result of my increasing girth, getting up and down the many stairs in our new house became harder and harder. I didn't realize it at the time, but my increased size wasn't just sapping my energy, it was putting a significant strain on my back as well.

Daisy and I got to sleep in our parents' big four-poster bed. Because the mattress was roughly three feet off of the floor, and since beagles aren't good jumpers, our parents stacked a series of thick mats on top of one another and formed steps for us to get on and off the bed. This arrangement worked great until one night when I foolishly elected to jump off the bed rather than use the steps they had provided. WHAT A MISTAKE!

The House of Many Steps

Beagles, like dachshunds, have a more fragile spinal column than most other breeds of dogs. Given my overweight condition and lack of jumping skills, when I hit the floor, I landed awkwardly, and felt a sudden and severe pain in my back. Though I could still limp around on all four legs my parents quickly realized that I needed immediate medical attention.

When we rushed into the veterinarian's office the next morning, the doctor took one look at me and said I needed surgery right away. He concluded that I had ruptured a disk in my back, and without an operation I might never walk again.

My sister had hurt her back the year before but got over her problem without surgery, so my parents asked if we could wait a day to see if my condition improved. They didn't want to make me go through surgery if it wasn't absolutely necessary. This proved to be another BIG MISTAKE. Instead of getting better I got worse – a lot worse. By the time we finally went forward with my operation, my chance for a full recovery had greatly diminished.

My recuperation from the operation proved to be long and difficult, and though I no longer experienced any kind of pain, I never did fully recover. My spine had been seriously damaged and though I still had feeling in my hind legs, I couldn't put any weight on them. As a result, I couldn't stand up and I couldn't walk around. Worse yet, I couldn't wag my tail. How was I going to convey my feelings to others if I couldn't wag my tail? How was I going to tell dogs I might meet in the park that I was a happy, fun-loving dog and wanted to be their friend? Life was clearly going to be different from this point on.

My mental state wasn't any better than my physical state. I became depressed and self-conscious about my limitations. No longer did I enjoy watching Animal Planet; no longer did I enjoy socializing with other dogs or doing things with my family. All I wanted to do was sleep.

In real years, I was five at the time of my accident. In dog years I was 35; a young adult with plenty of life to live. Instead of being able to walk around in the house, I would now have to get around by sliding on my rump while pulling myself with my front legs. At first this was quite a challenge, but the more I did it, the easier it became. Thank goodness we had slick hardwood floors and not wall-to-wall carpeting. (Had we the latter, I'm sure my rump would have been one big rug burn.)

While I was getting better at moving around in the house, I had to wonder how I was going to get around outside. How was I going to be able to go to the bathroom when I needed to? How was I going to slide around on the sidewalk and in the street without hurting myself?

Thank goodness for the internet! My Mom quickly found she could order a customized pull-cart for me from a company in Oak Harbor, Washington, that specializes in making mobile devices for animals that injure themselves, as I had. The one they made for me is called a K-9 cart (get it, a ca-nine cart).

My new set of wheels was much like a wheelchair. However, unlike a wheelchair, I didn't really sit in it. The cart had two donut-shaped, padded rings above the back two wheels. My two hind legs slipped through these padded rings which served to not only keep my two back paws from touching the ground, but gave good support to my rear end as well. It also had a support strap in front that went under my belly and another strap that went over the top of my back. These two straps served as a harness allowing me to pull the cart with my two good front legs.

In reality, my new rig was a lot more like a Chinese rickshaw. The only difference being that I was both the puller *and* the pullee. It goes without saying that once my new cart arrived my life became much less of a challenge – it got better, a lot better, and a lot more fun.

I couldn't use my cart in the house without constantly banging into furniture, but I sure could use it everywhere else. Now I could run in the park, on the beach, and wherever my front legs could pull me. I could even run after cars if I wanted to. Though I never did when I had four good legs because my parents always warned me of the danger and, like a good boy, I always listened to my parents. Granted, it was a little hard going up hills in my new cart, but on the other hand, it sure was easier and more exciting going down the other side.

With time, my self consciousness began to subside. I committed myself to leading as normal and active a life as possible. I WOULD OVERCOME! While I wouldn't be able to do everything I had done before, there would be new interests to pursue and new friends to make.

When my folks took me to the park or out for a walk, I would occasionally notice people staring at me. Apparently they had never seen a dog in a wheelchair before. Often, they would come over to pet me and ask my parents what had happened to me. This initially bothered me, but then I began to realize they admired my spirit, my spunk – they admired my positive attitude, my determination to put my problems behind me (no pun intended). What they saw was a frisky, friendly dog, intent with getting on with his life.

Thank Goodness for
Hardwood Floors

Ready to Roll

All the Comforts of Home

The Grass is Always Greener at the Park

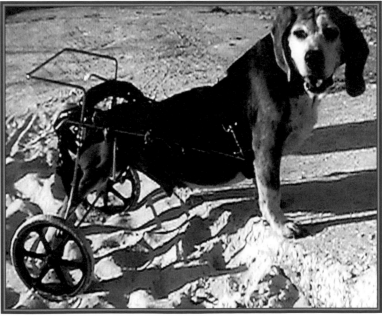

My New Set of Wheels

Scents, Scents, Everywhere a Scent

Barney the Beach Bum

My folks had a dog nanny who watched after Daisy and me when they went on vacation or were away on business. She was very impressed upon seeing my new set of wheels and wished all dog owners could be made aware of their availability should they ever need such a device for their pet.

After taking me for a walk and seeing how well my cart worked, and how easy it was to maneuver, she asked my Dad if he would mind if she contacted the local news media in the hope that they would do a story about my wonderful new wagon.

He said, "Please do!" as he was very excited about the improved quality of life I would now be enjoying and wanted pet lovers everywhere to know how they could get one, if needed.

That is how I became a well known television personality. Shortly after the local media was contacted two different reporters called my Dad to ask if they could do an interview. First, the city's major newspaper did a front-page story with a big picture of me in my cart. They tagged the article, "Dog On a Roll." Next, the local television station did a

45-second human interest piece for the evening news. It didn't stop there. Apparently this news feature was seen by producers from the national cable channel CNN and they picked up the piece to run on their daily news show, "HEADLINE NEWS."

As a result, I was seen by millions of viewers all over the country. And just as my Nanny had hoped, the stations that aired my story received calls from dog lovers everywhere who wanted to know how to order a similar cart for their injured pet. (I just wish such purchases, given their necessity, could be covered by some form of medical insurance. Maybe they could call it "Peticare.")

I was very pleased at the favorable response this news feature received. Now other physically challenged dogs, like myself, would be able to get carts of their own and start enjoying life more fully. Now, they too, would be able to run in the park, sniffing out their favorite smells. They too, would be able to scamper on the beach and frolic in the surf and perhaps, most importantly, would now be able to go outside and _go_ when they had to _go_!

They Thought Me Newsworthy,
The Front Page No Less

I Passed My Driver's Test with Flying Colors

Look Mom, I'm on TV!

Celebrating My Twelfth Birthday
(84 in Dog Years)

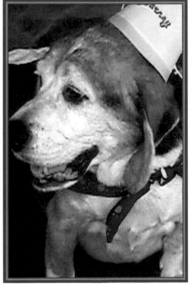

My New Girlfriend Molly,
One of Six Four-Legged
Guests
at My Party

Barney the
Party Animal

The message of my story is this; don't sell yourself short! Be all you can be! You too can overcome life's obstacles; but you have to be willing to work at it. It won't be easy, but then again, what in life is?

Out of my misfortune, a lot of good fortune has resulted for pets like me. This makes me very happy. And though I can't wag my tail to show you just how happy I am, just look into my eyes and you can see for yourself.

By way of an epilogue, Barney lived to be thirteen and a half (94 in dog years), and though he is gone, he will never be forgotten by his adopted parents, Bob and Judy Reintsema. His love for life, his friendly disposition and his ability to persevere in spite of his hardships has left an indelible mark on all who knew him. He was truly one of a kind.

CPSIA information can be obtained
at www.ICGtesting.com
Printed in the USA
LVXC01n1300270314
379130LV00001B/1